The Seven Secrets of Prayer

Chris Ojigbani

xulon PRESS

Copyright © 2015 by Chris Ojigbani

The Seven Secrets Of Prayer
by Chris Ojigbani

Printed in the United States of America.

ISBN 9781498458733

All rights reserved solely by the author. The author guarantees all contents are original and do not infringe upon the legal rights of any other person or work. No part of this book may be reproduced in any form without the permission of the author. The views expressed in this book are not necessarily those of the publisher.

Scripture quotations taken from the King James Version (KJV)
– *public domain*

The names of the persons in the testimonies in this book have been changed to protect their identities.

Singles and Married Ministries
9-11 Gunnery Terrace, Royal Arsenal, Woolwich
London SE18 6SW, England
Tel: +44 757 655 4405
www.singlesandmarried.org
info@singlesandmarried.org

www.xulonpress.com

Act 19 - 1 2-6

John 20 - 19-22

Ad 1 - 6-8

Ad 3 - 1 - 2-3-7

Act 5 - 15-16

DEDICATION

To the Glory of God

CONTENTS

CHAPTER 1
THE SEVEN SECRETS OF PRAYER 9

CHAPTER 2
FIRST SECRET 12

CHAPTER 3
SECOND SECRET. 31

CHAPTER 4
THIRD SECRET. 61

CHAPTER 5
FOURTH SECRET. 75

CHAPTER 6
FIFTH SECRET 88

CHAPTER 7
SIXTH SECRET..................102

CHAPTER 8
SEVENTH SECRET 119

CHAPTER 9
THE MOST POWERFUL
PROTECTION PRAYER POINT......134

CHAPTER 10
MY ADVICE 142

SHARE YOUR TESTIMONY 147

OTHER BOOKS WRITTEN BY
CHRIS OJIGBANI..................149

CHAPTER 1

THE SEVEN SECRETS OF PRAYER

"Pastor Chris, why is it that God hasn't answered my prayer for a good job?" Mikel once asked me. Mikel had prayed for a good job for over one year without result. He didn't understand why the prayer wasn't working, and that prompted him to ask me the question. There are many persons in Mikel's shoes. They are unhappy because they have prayed for a particular need time and time again without success.

So many persons suffering from illness have prayed time after time without being healed. A lot of singles have prayed for life partners year after year without success. Some families have prayed for children for years without any result. Many Christians have prayed time and time again without having their desires.

Why do many persons pray without having their desires? The answer is simply because they don't conform to the guidelines of prayer. Yes, prayer does have guidelines. And everyone who wants his prayers to produce results must conform to the guidelines. Though the guidelines of prayer are scriptural, they are secrets. They are mysteries: the hidden wisdom of God (1 Corinthians 2:7).

Whenever one lacks the knowledge of any mystery of God, he suffers in that area of life. But when one accesses a mystery of God, he excels in that area of life. If you want to receive answers to all your prayer points, then you must access the fundamental secrets of prayer.

No matter what you desire, your understanding of the fundamental secrets will completely guarantee answers to your prayers. Do you desire to marry easily? Are you already married and desire to be happy in marriage? Is it a healing miracle or a financial blessing you need? Do you desire a child? Or do you just want all your prayers to produce results? All you need to do is to access the fundamental secrets of prayer, and you will get answers to all your prayers. The whole essence of this book is to share with you the fundamental secrets as revealed to me by the Holy Spirit. I call them the seven secrets of prayer.

CHAPTER 2

FIRST SECRET

The first secret of a successful prayer is very important and shocking. It states that you should not pray to God, but rather pray to the Father. In other words, address God as Father anytime you pray. Though God is the same person as the Father, the two names don't have the same connotation. God refers to the creator and ruler of the universe, but the name Father signifies He has intimate father-child relationship with His children. Addressing Him as God does not indicate He has a relationship with you. On the other hand, addressing Him as Father does not only indicate He has an intimate father-child relationship with you, but also reminds Him of the relationship. **And the Father respects intimate relationship so much that anytime a person reminds Him of His intimate relationship, He goes out of His way to grant the person's prayer requests.**

Before the coming of Jesus Christ, God had intimate relationship with a few individuals on earth. He had a friendship relationship with Abraham (2 Chronicles 20:7). He also had master-servant relationship with very few people, including Abraham (Exodus 32:13). Though God didn't have intimate relationship with many persons, those who knew that He respects His intimate relationship still took advantage of it by reminding Him of His intimate relationship with Abraham. And that propelled God to answer their prayers. One such person was Jehoshaphat. When the vast army of Ammon, Moab and Mount Seir waged a war against him, he prayed unto the Lord for help. To make God grant his prayer request, he reminded Him of His friendship relationship with Abraham.

> Art not thou our God, who didst drive out the inhabitants of this land before thy people Israel, and gavest it to the seed of Abraham thy friend for ever?
> 2 Chronicles 20:7

Jehoshaphat knew that Abraham was God's friend and took advantage of it by reminding God of the intimate relationship. God granted his prayer request and even fought for him by making the three armies to kill themselves: not even one person escaped (2 Chronicles 20:22-24). God also granted the prayer requests of others who reminded Him of His intimate relationship with Abraham (Exodus 32:13-14,

Deuteronomy 9:26-10:2, 1 Chronicles 29:18-25, Genesis 32:9-11).

Prior to the death and resurrection of Christ, God had intimate relationship with a limited number of persons but He now has intimate father-child relationship with all believers. Presently, believers are sons of God (John 1:12). He is Our Father and we are His children. So, whenever you pray, all you need to do is to remind Him of His intimate relationship with you by addressing Him as Father. And He will grant your prayer request.

True Definition of Prayer

In Christianity, the correct definition of prayer is a communication between a child and the Father. It's not entirely correct to define prayer as a communication between man and God because we are now His children, and He is Our Father. At the present time, the Father has intimate father-child relationship with us. If He truly has intimate relationship with us, then the intimacy must reflect in our communication with Him. If He is truly Our Father, we must address Him as Father whenever we communicate with Him.

If your father were the president of your country, would you address him as Mr. President? No! You would definitely address him as father. Though he is the president of your country, he is still your father. People may call him Mr. President but you will call him father. If God is truly your heavenly Father, then you must address Him as Father. People may address Him as God, but you must call Him Father anytime you communicate with Him because He is your Father. Prayer is a communication where a child talks to the Father. Jesus also defined prayer as a communication between a child and the Father.

And it came to pass, that, as he was praying in a certain place, when he ceased, one of his disciples said unto him, Lord, teach us to pray, as John also taught his disciples.

And he said unto them, When ye pray, say, Our Father which art in heaven.

Luke 11:1-2

In the above scripture, Jesus taught us how to pray. He said that when we pray, we should say "Our Father which art in heaven". Take note that He didn't teach us to say "Our God which art in heaven". Rather, He taught us to say "Our Father which art in heaven". In other words, He wants us to direct our prayers to our heavenly Father. Yes, He wants us to communicate with the Father. And for Jesus to teach us to address Him as Father means that He wants us to communicate with Him as His children. If we address Him as Father, then we are His children. **So, Jesus' definition of prayer is a communication between a child and the Father.** That is the simple truth!

When you address Him as Father, you not only remind Him of His intimate father-child relationship with you, you also remind Him of His responsibility to protect and care for you. It's a father's responsibility to care for his children and give them their hearts' desires. Every father gives good gifts to his children.

> Or what man is there of you, whom if his son ask bread, will he give him a stone?
>
> Or if he ask a fish, will he give him a serpent?
>
> If ye then, being evil, know how to give good gifts unto your children, how much more shall your Father which is

in heaven give good things to them that ask him?

> Matthew 7:9-11

If men, as evil as they are, know how to give good gifts to their children, then our heavenly Father, as good as He is, will give good gifts to those who ask Him. In simple words, if men give good gifts to their children, then our heavenly Father will definitely give good gifts to His children who ask Him. When you address Him as Father, you remind Him of His responsibility to care for you. And He will in turn give you good gifts. Fathers give good gifts to their children.

Sometime ago, when my daughter was a little above one, my wife and I went with her to get some grocery from a shop in Kent England. My daughter picked a toy from the shop's toy stand and my wife quickly asked her to drop it, as we didn't have any intention of buying one that day. But my daughter, who obviously liked the toy, didn't want to drop it. As my wife tried grabbing it from her, she shouted "Dad". I was really touched when I heard her scream "Dad". It reminded me of my responsibility to care for her. And that propelled me to buy her the toy. Though I didn't have any intention of buying a toy that day, I bought my daughter one because she called me Dad. Addressing God as Father not only reminds Him of His intimate relationship with you, but also reminds Him of His responsibility to care for you. And that will in turn propel Him to grant your prayer request, even when you don't deserve it. It's a secret!

How did Jesus address God in Prayer?

Jesus Christ addressed God as Father in all His prayers. He never addressed Him as God in any of His prayers. He had access to this first secret of prayer and fully utilized it. He recognized His intimate relationship with God and addressed God as Father every time He prayed. No wonder all His prayers produced wonderful results.

> At that time Jesus answered and said, I thank thee, O Father, Lord of heaven and earth, because thou hast hid these things from the wise and prudent, and hast revealed them unto babes.
> Matthew 11:25

In the scripture above, Jesus addressed God as Father in prayer. Though He referred to God as the Lord of the heavens and the earth, He still emphasized His intimate relationship with God by addressing Him as Father.

And he was withdrawn from them about a stone's cast, and kneeled down, and prayed,

Saying, Father, if thou be willing, remove this cup from me: nevertheless not my will, but thine, be done.
>Luke 22:41-42

In Jesus' prayer above, He also addressed God as Father. It's not a sin to address Him as God, but if you want your prayers to produce results, you must start addressing Him as Father every time you pray.

Then said Jesus, Father, forgive them; for they know not what they do. And they parted his raiment, and cast lots.
>Luke 23:34

First Secret

Jesus addressed God as Father when He prayed for the forgiveness of those who crucified Him. Even when He raised Lazarus from the dead, He also directed His prayers to our heavenly Father.

> Then they took away the stone from the place where the dead was laid. And Jesus lifted up his eyes, and said, Father, I thank thee that thou hast heard me.
>
> John 11:41

All Jesus' prayers in the Bible were actually addressed to the Father. **If Jesus addressed God as Father in all His prayers, it simply means that the right way of praying is to address God as Father.** It also means that Jesus wants us to address God as Father every time we pray. From now onwards, ensure you address Him as Father every time you pray. When you address Him as Father, you not only remind Him of His intimate relationship with you, you also remind Him of His responsibility to protect and care for you. And that will propel Him to give you your heart's desires. **At this point, I must warn that everyone does not have the right to address God as Father.** To be eligible to address God as Father, there are two conditions you must meet.

First Condition

For you to be eligible to address God as Father, you must have a relationship with Him, and the relationship must be intimate.

How can one develop a relationship with God?

One can develop a relationship with God by becoming a child of God. And the only means of becoming a child of God is through

First Secret

Jesus Christ (John 14:6). Apart from Jesus, there is no other name under heaven by which one can be saved (Acts 4:12). When one confesses that Jesus is the Lord and believes in his heart that God raised Him from the dead, he is automatically saved (Romans 10:9). And the moment he is saved, he becomes a child of God and develops a relationship with God. This explains why the Bible says that to those who believed in His name, He gave the power to become sons of God (John 1:12). It's only by faith in Christ that we are children of God (Galatians 3:26).

So, if you want to develop a relationship with God, all you need to do is to confess that Jesus is the Lord and believe in your heart that God raised Him from the dead. And when you develop a relationship with God, make sure it's intimate.

How can one ensure his relationship with God is intimate?

Abstinence from sin makes a relationship with God to be intimate. A true child of God does not commit sin (1 John 3:7). When a child of God abstains from sin, his relationship with God becomes intimate. But if he indulges in sin, God becomes distant with him. God is always very distant with sinners. Though we live in the dispensation of grace, you must abstain from sin for your relationship with God to be intimate. That we are under grace does not imply you have the liberty to commit sin. Rather, it does imply that the dominion of sin over you has been destroyed (Romans 6:14).

Second Condition

The second condition you must meet to have the right to address God as Father is the understanding of what it really means to be a child of God. If God is truly your Father, then you must have the right knowledge of what it means. Anyone who lacks the right knowledge in the Kingdom suffers (Hosea 4:6). When a child of God lacks the right knowledge of what it really means to be a child of God, he loses the benefits and suffers as if he is not a child of God.

Understanding what it means to be a child of God

There are three kinds of intimate relationship one can have with God. One can be a servant of God, a friend of God, or a child of God. Amongst these three, being a child of God is the most intimate. Being a child of God is the most intimate relationship anyone can ever have with God. It's a great privilege we must never take for granted.

Before the coming of Christ, God had intimate master-servant relationship with a few persons on earth, including Abraham. (Exodus 32:13. God also had an intimate friendship relationship with Abraham (2 Chronicles 20:7). But after the death and resurrection of Jesus, the Son of God, a new kind of intimate relationship with God was birthed. It's called a son of God relationship or a child of God relationship. Now, anyone who believes in Jesus Christ, becomes a son of God in the same manner Jesus is the Son of God (John 1:12). As children of God, our relationship with God is exactly the same kind of relationship Christ has with God. This is the reason, immediately after His resurrection, Jesus referred to His disciples as His brothers.

> Jesus said, "Do not hold on to me, for I have not yet ascended to the Father. Go instead to **my brothers** and tell them, 'I

am ascending to **my Father and your Father**, to my God and your God.'"

John 20:17 (NIV)

In the scripture above, after His death and resurrection, Jesus referred to His disciples as His brothers. Initially, Jesus' disciples were His servants. Later on, the relationship changed and they became His friends (John 15:15). But after His resurrection, in the scripture above, the relationship changed again and they became His brothers. **So, believers are now Jesus' brothers.** And because we are His brothers, we also have a common Father. His Father is Our Father. This explains why Jesus said in the above scripture that His Father was equally His disciples' Father. **If you are truly a disciple of Christ, then God is your Father in the same manner He is Jesus' Father.** God sees you in the same way He sees Jesus. He also loves you in the same way

He loves Jesus. It's the understanding of this very intimate relationship with the Father that will give rise to the success of your prayers.

If you don't have a relationship with God, develop it now. If you already have one, abstain from sin and the relationship will become intimate. As long as you have an intimate relationship with the Father, and you truly understand what it means to be a child of God, address Him as Father when you pray. And your prayers will produce results. It's a powerful secret that makes prayer work.

CHAPTER 3

SECOND SECRET

The second secret of prayer is a spiritual law that cannot be altered. It states that so long as you pray believing, the Father will grant all your prayer requests that are according to your will. In other words, your prayer points do not have to be according to God's will before your prayers will produce results. Rather, your prayers will definitely produce results even when all your prayer points are according to your own will, provided that you pray believing. So, you will have your will, and not God's will, if you pray believing. This secret is so important in the Kingdom that when one lacks the knowledge, it hinders him from getting answers to his prayers. Though the secret is scriptural, very many persons are unaware of it because it's hidden. Even when some persons read the scriptures that contain the secret, they still don't understand it because it's hidden. Before showing you the scriptural references for this second secret of prayer, I will first correct an error existing in the Christian community.

God Does Not Grant Only Prayer Requests that are according to His Will

There is absolutely no limit to what one can achieve through prayer, provided that he prays believing. But unfortunately, many persons are of the opinion that God answers one's prayer only if what he asks for is in accordance with His will. They share such opinion mainly because they misinterpret the scripture below.

> And this is the confidence that we have in him, that, if we ask any thing according to his will, he heareth us.
> 1 John 5:14

Though many Bible translators have rendered the above scripture to mean that God hears us only if the particular thing we ask for is in accordance with His will, that's not correct. The actual meaning of the scripture is that God hears us if our asking for a thing is according to His will. The scripture is talking about the way and manner we ask for a thing, and not about the particular thing we ask for. It's talking about the asking itself. The scripture means that God hears us if our asking is according to His will. What is God's will in asking? God's will in asking is that we should ask believing and must not doubt (James 1:5-7). Below is the correct rendering of the scripture.

> The confidence we have in Him is that if we ask anything believing, He hears us.

The major reason people misinterpret the scripture is because they read it in isolation. If you read the scripture together with the next verse, it will be easier to understand.

> And this is the confidence that we have in him, that, if we ask any thing according to his will, he heareth us.
>
> And if we know that he hear us, whatsoever we ask, we know that we have the petitions that we desired of him.
> 1 John 5:14-15

Verse 15 above plainly says that if we know God hears us, we will receive "whatsoever" we ask for. The word "whatsoever" in the passage is not limited to things that are according to God's will. It means anything at all: including things that are not according to God's will. If verse 15 says we will receive things that are not according to God's will, it simply means that verse 14 does not say we will receive only things that are according to God's will. The two verses cannot contradict themselves. Below is the correct rendering of the scripture in verses 14 and 15 put together.

The confidence we have in Him is that if we ask anything believing, He hears us.

And if we know that He hears us, whatever we ask Him, we know that He has granted.

God grants all our prayer requests, provided that we ask believing. He does not grant only the prayer requests that are in accordance with His will. **Praying for things that are according to God's will is not the key to success in prayer. This explains why so many persons pray for things that are according to God's will and still don't have their hearts' desires.** The key to successful prayer is to ask believing. So long as you ask believing, you will have whatever you want.

The Scriptural Basis for the Secret

There are actually many scriptural references for this secret of prayer. Though many persons are conversant with the scriptures that contain the secret, they are still unaware of the secret because it's truly hidden. Let's first look at a scripture in the Book of Mark where Jesus Christ Himself revealed the secret.

Therefore I say unto you, What things soever ye desire, when ye pray, believe that ye receive them, and ye shall have them.

Mark 11:24

In the above scripture, Jesus clearly said that we will have "what things soever" we desire, provided that we pray believing. First, "what things soever" in the passage means anything at all. Second, "your desire" in the passage means the same thing as "your will". So, the rendering of the scripture above is:

Therefore I say to you, no matter what your will is, you will have it, so long as you pray believing.

Before the coming of Jesus, people didn't know it was their right to have their will. But in the above scripture, Jesus revealed that we will have our will, provided that we pray believing. Jesus was the first person to reveal this powerful secret. It is a law: a spiritual law. If Jesus said it, then it's the truth. He couldn't have lied. It's the simple truth. No matter how far-fetched your will seems to be, you will surely have it, provided that you pray believing. There is another interesting scripture where Jesus revealed the same secret.

> "'If you can'?" said Jesus. "Everything is possible for one who believes."
>
> Mark 9:23 (NIV)

The scripture above is very correct. If you pray believing, all things will be possible for you. "Everything" in the scripture means anything at all: including things that are not according to God's will. **When a child of God believes, he automatically operates like a supernatural being and no goal will**

Second Secret

be impossible for him to achieve. If you want your prayers to produce results, you must understand that it's your right to have whatever you want, provided that you pray believing. The plain truth is that no power is strong enough to stop you from having your will, when you pray believing. **Even if your will is contrary to God's will, you will still have it, as long as you pray believing.** This explains why Jesus had to voluntarily pray for God's will to be done when He asked the Father to remove the cup of suffering from Him.

> Saying, Father, if thou be willing, remove this cup from me: nevertheless not my will, but thine, be done.
>
> Luke 22:42

Just before Jesus' arrest that led to His suffering and crucifixion, He shrank from the horror of the Cross. And in the scripture above, He asked the Father to remove the cup of suffering and crucifixion from Him. Notwithstanding, He also prayed that the Father's will, and not His will, should prevail. The Father's will was for Jesus to be crucified while Jesus' will was for the Father to stop His suffering and crucifixion by taking away the cup from Him.

Jesus had the understanding that anyone who prays believing will have his will. Therefore, of His own accord, He prayed that His own will shouldn't happen. He allowed the Father's will to prevail. Though He wanted the cup to be removed from Him, He voluntarily allowed the Father's will to prevail.

For Jesus to voluntarily pray that His own will shouldn't happen simply means that His will could actually happen. If His will couldn't happen, He wouldn't have prayed that it shouldn't happen. Though His will was

Second Secret

contrary to the Father's will, it could happen. **If Jesus' will that was contrary to the Father's will could happen, it confirms that a prayer point doesn't have to be in accordance with the Father's will before the prayer will produce results.** It also confirms that a prayer can still produce result even when the prayer point is contrary to the "Father's will". That's the simple truth. Do you know that the whole essence of prayer is to petition the Father for our will to happen? Yes, you don't need to petition the Father for His will to happen.

Why Do We Pray?

The whole essence of prayer is to petition the Father for our will to happen. In other words, we petition the Father because we desire something. You don't need to petition the Father for Him to have His desire. When you pray for God's will, it actually means you are praying for the Father to have His desire. But you don't need to pray for the Father. He does not need your prayer. You cannot intercede on His behalf. He is the King of Kings. When you petition the Father, it should be for your own needs, and not for His needs. If we don't need to petition the Father for His needs, why did Jesus pray for the Father's will to happen?

Why Jesus prayed for the Father's will to Happen

> Saying, Father, if thou be willing, remove this cup from me: nevertheless not my will, but thine, be done.
>
> Luke 22:42

Jesus prayed for the Father's will to happen because He had already asked the Father to stop His crucifixion by taking away the cup from Him. So, knowing that the Father would grant His request and stop the crucifixion, He voluntarily prayed for the Father's will to happen.

If Jesus had not asked the Father to take away the cup from Him, He wouldn't have had any need to pray for the Father's will to happen. The Father's will, which was for Jesus to be crucified, would have just happened. In prayer, we don't need to petition the Father for His needs. Why then did Jesus say we should pray for the Father's will to be done on earth?

What does "Thy will be done, as in heaven, so in earth" mean?

Jesus Christ taught that we should ask Our Father, amongst other things, for His will to be done on earth as in heaven.

Thy will be done, as in heaven, so in earth.

Luke 11:2

The scripture above means that we should ask our heavenly Father for His will to be done on earth in the same manner it is done in heaven. In other words, Jesus wants us to pray for human beings to start doing the Father's will just like the heavenly beings do the Father's will. The scripture does not mean that you should petition the Father for His needs. It simply means that we should pray for human beings to start behaving well: to start doing God's will on earth.

You don't need to petition the Father for His needs. In prayer, you petition the Father for your own needs. And whenever you petition Him, ensure you pray believing. So long as you pray believing, your prayer will be successful. Belief is a prerequisite for successful prayer. If belief is this important, what does it mean to believe?

What does it mean to Believe?

To have a full understanding of what it means to believe, it's important we revisit the scripture where Jesus said that we will have whatever we desire, if we pray believing.

> Therefore I say unto you, What things soever ye desire, when ye pray, believe that ye receive them, and ye shall have them.
> Mark 11:24

"Believe" in the above scripture comes from the Greek word "pisteuo", and it means to have complete and total confidence in the Lord. So, the scripture above means that if you have complete and total confidence in

God that He has already granted your prayer requests, you will then have whatever you desire. It simply means that you must first have confidence that God has answered your prayers before you can receive answers to your prayers. How can you have confidence anytime you pray?

How to Develop Confidence in Prayer

Confidence is determined by the state of a person's heart. For you to have confidence that God has answered your prayers, your heart must not condemn you. If your heart doesn't condemn you, you will have confidence before God and will then receive answers to your prayers.

> Beloved, if our heart condemn us not, then have we confidence toward God.

And whatsoever we ask, we receive of him.

1 John 3:21-22a

The scripture above clearly explains that if our hearts don't condemn us, we will have confidence toward God and receive whatever we ask for. So, the state of one's heart determines whether he will have confidence or not. If your heart condemns you, you cannot have confidence. But if your heart does not condemn you, you will then have confidence.

What causes a man's heart to condemn him?

When one disobeys and displeases God, his heart will condemn him, and he can no longer have confidence before God. But when one does the things that please God, his heart will not condemn him.

Beloved, if our heart condemn us not, then have we confidence toward God.

And whatsoever we ask, we receive of him, because we keep his commandments, and do those things that are pleasing in his sight.

1 John 3:21-22

The scripture above says that if our hearts don't condemn us, we will have confidence before God and receive whatever we ask because we keep His commandments and do the things that please Him. In other words, if you keep His commandments and do the things that please Him, your heart won't condemn you when you pray. On the other hand, when you disobey and displease God, your heart will condemn you and you won't have confidence before God.

If you want to receive whatever you pray for, you must keep God's commandments and do the things that please Him. When you keep His commandments, your heart won't condemn you. Because your heart does not condemn you, you will have confidence before God. The confidence will then empower you to receive answers to your prayers. So, the key to success in prayer is to have confidence before God, that is, to pray believing. No matter how far-fetched your desires seem to be, you will have them, provided that you pray believing. Mama's testimony will inspire you.

Mama's Testimony

Mama, as she is fondly called, was 68 years old when she came to my office for counseling on November 28, 2009. Although she had never been married, she was a grandmother. She had a son when she was in secondary school. Her son, who was 49 years old, was married with two children: a girl and a boy. Mama's granddaughter was 21 years old while her grandson was 14 years old.

Mama came to my office for counseling on that fateful day and said something that surprised me. When I first saw her, I thought that she had come to seek for counsel for her daughter or granddaughter. But to my greatest surprise, mama said to me "Pastor, I am lonely. I desire to marry". I summoned up courage to counsel her, but my faith was really challenged when it was time to pray for her. Though I had been praying for people and they had been getting married easily, they were not as old as Mama. I wondered how she would be able to get married at age 68. I became really scared that my prayer might not produce results. And at that instant, a soft voice spoke to my heart "My son, don't worry yourself. Just pray for her and I will bring it to pass". I was encouraged by the voice and I prayed for her believing.

Mama left my office encouraged. The following week, on Saturday December 5, 2009, she attended our seminar at the Muson Centre Lagos Nigeria and had an amazing miracle. At the seminar, God orchestrated a 69-year-old man to sit beside Mama. At the end of the seminar, the 69-year-old man exchanged phone numbers with her. They started corresponding, and few weeks later, He proposed marriage to her. When Mama gave her testimony at our seminar, some young ladies at the seminar were so amazed that they shed tears. It was amazing!

Mama had such amazing miracle because I prayed for her believing. Initially, I doubted if the prayer could produce results. But after the soft voice of the Holy Spirit encouraged me, I believed. I then prayed for her believing, and the prayer produced amazing results. No matter what you desire, you will surely have it, provided that you pray believing. Matilda's testimony will also inspire you.

Matilda's Testimony

Matilda was in her mid thirties when she attended our seminar at the Phoenix Event Centre Houston Texas, USA on July 3, 2015. She was happily married but was troubled because she discovered she had a lump in her breast. She then decided to attend our seminar to seek for divine healing.

Matilda's faith was strengthened after listening to my teaching on how one can achieve his goals through prayer. During the prayer session, she prayed believing and the lump in her breast disappeared instantly. Whenever one prays believing, he gets whatever he wants. Clement also prayed believing and got married effortlessly.

Clement's Testimony

Clement desired to marry but experienced difficulty in finding the kind of lady he wanted to marry. The ladies he liked didn't like him, and the ones who liked him, he didn't like. It was a serious issue for him because he didn't want to make a mistake in his choice of spouse.

Clement continued experiencing difficulty in finding his right spouse until he attended our seminar at the Accra Sports Stadium Ghana on January 25, 2013. At the seminar, he did not just learn how to pray believing, he also practiced it. And he met a lady he liked right at the seminar. This time around, the lady liked him as well. They exchanged numbers and continued corresponding. Few months later, he proposed marriage to her. She accepted and they got married effortlessly.

Provided that you pray believing, you will have whatever you want. Belief is the determinant of the success of your prayer. When your belief is strengthened, you will surely pray believing, and your prayers will produce results. But when your belief is weakened, you will pray doubting, and the disbelief will in turn hinder your prayers from producing results. Unfortunately, many persons whose belief has already been weakened are not even aware of it. So, I consider it necessary to explain the factors that weaken belief.

Factors that weaken Belief

Many person's prayers don't produce results because their belief has been weakened. In this section, I will expose the factors that weaken belief.

Second Secret

First Factor that weakens Belief

Sin weakens a man's belief and hinders his prayers from producing results. When one indulges in sin, his heart condemns him and weakens his belief. Such person will definitely pray doubting, and the disbelief will automatically hinder his prayers from producing results.

For instance, if a man makes some prayer requests right after indulging in a sexual sin, his heart will condemn him, and he will pray doubting. The doubt will then hinder his prayers from producing results. Sin is a major hindrance to successful prayer.

Second Factor that weakens Belief

Apart from sin, another factor that weakens belief is asking God for something evil. Though we have the right to ask God for anything, asking for something evil weakens belief. When one prays for something bad, his heart will condemn him and he will pray doubting. The disbelief will then hinder him from having his heart's desire.

For instance, if a man prays for someone else to die, his heart will surely condemn him, and he won't believe God has answered his prayers. The disbelief will then hinder his prayer from producing results.

Third Factor that weakens Belief

The third factor that weakens belief is praying with wrong motives. When the motive behind a person's prayer is wrong, the person's heart will condemn him and weaken his belief. Such person will then pray doubting, and the disbelief will in turn hinder the success of his prayer. This explains why the Bible says that praying with wrong motives hinders the success of prayer (James 4:3).

Even when a person prays for a good thing, his heart will still condemn him, if the motive behind the prayer is wrong. For instance, if a married man prays for financial blessing so that he can travel to a far country for an extramarital affair, his heart will surely condemn him. Though asking for financial blessing is not a sin, the motive behind the asking is wrong. Because the motive is wrong, his heart will condemn him and weaken his belief. As a result of that, his prayer will not produce results.

Fourth Factor that weakens Belief

The fourth factor that weakens belief is the wrong popular opinion that the Father answers one's prayer only if what he asks for is in accordance with His will. When one who shares such opinion prays, he will wonder whether his prayer point is in accordance with God's will or not. The person may end up doubting the efficacy of his prayer. As a result of the doubt, his prayer won't produce results (James 1:5-7).

Some persons suffering from illness are still ill today because they are not sure it's God's will for them to be healed. If you need healing, you must believe that God wants you to be healed because the Bible says I wish above all things that you will prosper and have good health (3 John 1:2).

There are so many people who pray for God's direction to their right spouses but are still single today because they are not sure it's God's will for them to marry. If you are not yet married, you must know that God is not against your marriage because He said that it's not good for a man to be alone (Genesis 2:18).

Your prayers will produce results, not because your prayer points are in accordance

Second Secret

with God's will, but because you pray believing. Regardless of what you desire, you will have it, so long as you pray believing. Belief is the determinant of the success of your prayer. So, ensure that your belief is not weakened. Rather, see that it is strengthened. When your belief is strengthened, you will surely pray believing. And your prayers will in turn produce results.

To strengthen your belief, you must avoid the factors that weaken belief. First, you must abstain from sin. Second, do not ask God for something evil. Third, do not pray with wrong motives. Fourth, you need to fully comprehend the fact that when you pray believing, the Father will answer all your prayer points that are according to your will. If you can successfully avoid the factors that weaken belief, your belief will surely be strengthened. It will in turn empower you to pray believing, and your prayers will produce amazing results. It's a secret that cannot be altered.

CHAPTER 4

THIRD SECRET

This is a very interesting secret. It states that you must not speak much in prayer. Beloved, if you want your prayers to produce results, never you speak much in prayer. Do you know that it's a sin to speak much in prayer? Yes, Jesus Christ cautioned us to desist from speaking much in prayer.

> But when ye pray, use not vain repetitions, as the heathen do: for they think that they shall be heard for their much speaking.

Be not ye therefore like unto them: for your Father knoweth what things ye have need of, before ye ask him.

Matthew 6:7-8

In the above scripture, Jesus warned us never to use vain repetitions like the heathens. He further cautioned us never to be like the heathens who believed that the Father would hear their prayers for their much speaking. The scripture above clearly indicates that Jesus doesn't want us to speak much in prayer. People actually speak much in prayer because they don't believe that the Father hears them. So, they repeat their prayer points with the intention that the Father would eventually hear them. But Jesus said in the above scripture that the Father already knows your prayer point even before you ask Him.

For the fact that we are required to pray without ceasing (1 Thessalonians 5:17) doesn't mean you should repeat your prayer points at the same instant. Imagine if someone needs a cup of water from you and says "Please give me a cup of water, a cup of water, a cup of water. I say give me a cup of water, a cup of water…" You may actually feel that there is something wrong with him because of the way and manner he repeats his need. When you pray, you must realize that you are not talking to yourself. Rather, you are talking to someone: Our Father. It's also important you know that Our Father is not deaf. He hears very well. If human beings hear, then Our Father who created us hears as well. He hears excellently well. If you know that He hears, then you don't need to repeat your prayer point at the same instant. He actually knows what you need even before you ask Him (Matthew 6:8). I must state here that vain repetition is not the same thing as persistent prayer.

What is Persistent Prayer?

A persistent prayer is the act of asking Our Father for the same thing at different occasions. A typical example of persistent prayer is when one asks the Father for direction to a right spouse at 6 a.m. on a Monday, still prays the same prayer the next day and everyday until he gets his desired result. Another good example of persistent prayer is when Jesus prayed for the same thing every hour at three different occasions (Matthew 26:37-44). There is nothing wrong with persistent prayer. Jesus actually admonished us to pray persistently (Luke 18:1-8).

What is vain repetition?

A vain repetition is the act of asking Our Father for the same thing repeatedly at the same occasion. An example of vain repetition is when one asks the Father for direction to a right spouse repeatedly at the same time. A man may pray thus "Father please direct me to a right spouse. I want a right spouse. Father, direct me to a right spouse, a right spouse, a right spouse. Father, direct me to a right spouse, a right spouse". While there is nothing wrong with persistent prayer, vain repetition is wrong. It indicates lack of faith.

Vain repetition indicates lack of faith

When one repeats his prayer point at the same occasion, it's really an indication such person doesn't have faith, and the person should not expect to receive any good thing from the Lord (James 1:5-7). Most people's prayers don't produce results because they repeat their prayer points at the same occasion. If you believe Our Father hears, then there will be no need to repeat a prayer point. If you are sure Our Father hears, just go straight to the point and tell Him what you want. When Jesus was on earth, He said very short prayers.

Jesus said Short Prayers

Jesus Christ made use of this secret of prayer while on earth. He didn't speak much in prayer. He knew that Our Father hears very well, and that was why His said very short prayers. Most of His prayers were one-sentence prayers. He said one of such prayers shortly before His arrest.

> And he was withdrawn from them about a stone's cast, and kneeled down, and prayed,
>
> Saying, Father, if thou be willing, remove this cup from me: nevertheless not my will, but thine, be done.
>
> Luke 22:41-42

The prayer of Jesus above was a very important one. It was too important that Jesus had to withdraw from His disciples to pray in private. Though the prayer was very important, He still didn't speak much in the prayer. It was just a short one-sentence prayer: "Father, if thou be willing, remove this cup from me: nevertheless not my will, but thine, be done". Despite the fact that the prayer was very short, the Father heard Him instantly. How do I know that the Father heard Him instantly? The next verse tells us that an angel appeared immediately from heaven and strengthened Him.

And there appeared an angel unto him from heaven, strengthening him.
Luke 22:43

The scripture above indicates that we don't have to speak much in prayer before God hears us. He hears us even before we

speak. When Jesus was crucified, He also said a one-sentence forgiveness prayer for those who crucified Him.

> Then said Jesus, Father, forgive them; for they know not what they do.
>
> Luke 23:34

Jesus really made use of this secret of prayer. He said very effective short prayers. His prayers were short but very effective. What is the key to an effective short prayer?

Key to Effective Short Prayer

Belief is simply the key. When one believes that the Father hears him, his prayers will not just be short but very effective as well. People speak much in prayer because of disbelief: they don't believe that the Father hears them. And for that reason, they speak much in prayer with the hope that the Father will eventually hear them (Matthew 6:7-8). But when one believes that the Father hears him, he won't need to repeat his prayers. Such person will end up speaking less in prayer, and his prayers will be effective. **So, the more you believe, the less you speak in prayer. And the less you speak in prayer, the more effective your prayers.** Belief is the key. If belief is the key, how can you strengthen your belief?

To strengthen your belief, put into practice the four factors I explained in the previous chapter. Abstain from sin and do the things that please the Father (1 John 3:21-22). The second factor is to avoid asking the Father for something evil. You also need to pray with good motives. And lastly, you must believe that the Father answers all your prayers.

Strengthen your belief, and you will speak less in prayer. When you grow in faith, you will speak less in prayer, and your prayers will be effective. **The measure of your faith is inversely proportional to the measure of the time you spend in prayer.** The less your faith, the more time you spend in making prayer request. On the contrary, **the more your faith, the less time you spend in making prayer request. And the less time you spend in making prayer request, the more effective your prayer.** You can spend much time in the Word. You can also spend much time in worshiping or praising the Father. But if you grow in faith, you will spend less time in making prayer requests, and your prayers will be effective. At our seminars, we spend much time in the Word and in worship but we don't waste time in making prayer requests, and yet amazing miracles take place. What happened at our seminar at the Civic Centre Port Harcourt in January 2015 clearly confirms that short prayers really produce amazing and wonderful results. I named it the Civic Centre Miracles.

Civic Centre Miracles

We held a 2-Day powerful seminar at the Civic Centre Port Harcourt Nigeria on January 30 and February 1, 2015, and it was a huge success. The first day of the seminar was a night vigil, which started at 9pm. On that night, the 5000-seater hall was filled to capacity.

We spent much time to praise and worship the Father. We actually worshiped and danced for the Father for hours. It was so awesome that you could physical see the manifestation of His glory. The Word, which was with power, was for hours as well. After the Word, we worshiped the Father again. We then made prayer requests for about 10 minutes. And diverse kinds of amazing miracles took place. When I made alter call for testimonies, hundreds of persons came out.

The testimonies were so many that we didn't have enough time to take all that night. Many persons who were deaf regained their hearing. Some unmarried persons met their would-be spouses at the seminar. And so many others had diverse miracles. The key testimony of the night was a lady who was healed of a lump in her breast. She had earlier gone for a scan and the scan result confirmed that she had a lump in her breast. But during the short prayer session, the lump disappeared from her breast, and she couldn't feel it anymore. She came out and gave the testimony, and I asked her to go for another scan to confirm the lump was no longer there. She went for the second scan after the night vigil ended on Saturday morning and the scan confirmed that the lump no longer existed in her breast. She also came with both results to our seminar the next day. The atmosphere was electric when she showed the first scan result confirming a lump in her breast and the second scan result confirming the lump had disappeared. I cannot forget what happened on that day. It was really amazing!

We did not spend much time in prayer at the seminar and yet we recorded hundreds of amazing testimonies. Spending much time in prayer does not make prayers produce results. Rather, it stops prayers from producing results. If you want your prayers to produce results, then never you speak much in prayer. Never you repeat your prayer points. **Our Father is not deaf. When you repeat your prayer points, you actually imply that He doesn't hear well. You end up annoying Him.**

Build up your belief and speak less in prayer. Anytime you pray, always go straight to the point and tell the Father what you need. After telling Him what you need, you must believe that He has heard you. If you truly believe He has heard you, then you don't need to repeat your prayer point. In that manner, you will receive whatever you ask for. It's a secret of prayer: a very interesting secret.

CHAPTER 5

FOURTH SECRET

~~~~~~~~~~~~~~~

Speaking God's Word is the fourth secret. This secret is a very deep secret of prayer. When you return God's Word to Him in prayer, He hastens to perform it. Belief is a very important secret of prayer but you have to go a step further by speaking what you believe.

> We having the same spirit of faith, according as it is written, I believed, and therefore have I spoken; we also believe, and therefore speak.
>
> 2 Corinthians 4:13

After believing with your heart, the confession of your mouth is required for your salvation. For the fact that you are a child of God doesn't mean you will succeed in life automatically. If you want salvation in any area of life, you need to confess it.

> For with the heart man believeth unto righteousness; and with the mouth confession is made unto salvation.
>
> Romans 10:10

The above scripture says that the mouth is used for confession unto salvation. So, if you want the salvation of health, the confession of your mouth is required. If you want the salvation of finance or marriage, the confession of your mouth is necessary. If there is any area of your life you need the touch of God, start confessing what you want and it shall manifest effortlessly.

Fourth Secret

With the words of your mouth, you create your world. God created the world with His words (Hebrews 11:3). By speaking what you believe, you create your world. **Don't allow your situation to determine your words. Rather, change your situation with your words.** No matter how bad your situation may be, find out what the Bible says concerning the situation and start speaking it. And when you start confessing it, don't stop until your situation changes. It's a deep secret of success.

> This book of the law shall not depart out of thy mouth; but thou shalt meditate therein day and night, that thou mayest observe to do according to all that is written therein: for then thou shalt make thy way prosperous, and then thou shalt have good success.
>
> Joshua 1:8

The above scripture says that if you want to be prosperous and succeed in your endeavors, God's Word shall not depart from your mouth. In other words, you shall confess it every time. The scripture says you shall "meditate" on God's Word day and night and observe to do what the Word says. The Hebrew rendering of the word "meditate" in the scripture is "Hagah" and it means to ponder, to mutter, to speak, and to roar. To ponder means to think about something, to mutter means to speak in a very low and barely audible voice, to speak means to say something, while to roar means a loud and deep sound. So, apart from pondering on God's Word, the scripture above wants you to mutter God's Word, to speak God's Word and to roar God's Word.

Find out what God's Word says concerning your situation and start speaking it every now and then. If you are in a public place like the office, you can mutter it. But when you are in your house or in the church, you can speak it or even roar it. When you continuously speak into your situation, you will definitely have good success. A similar scripture can be found in the Book of Psalms as well.

> Blessed is the man that walketh not in the counsel of the ungodly, nor standeth in the way of sinners, nor sitteth in the seat of the scornful.
>
> But his delight is in the law of the Lord; and in his law doth he meditate day and night.
>
> And he shall be like a tree planted by the rivers of water, that bringeth forth his fruit in his season; his leaf also shall not wither; and whatsoever he doeth shall prosper.
>
> Psalms 1:1-3

The scripture above says that a godly man who "meditates" on God's Word day and night will prosper in whatever he does. The Hebrew rendering of the word "meditate" in the scripture above also means "hagah", and it means to ponder, to mutter, to speak, and to roar. Speaking God's Word is a very good way of succeeding in life. If there is any unpleasant situation in your life, you must start speaking to it. It's wrong to just keep quiet and cry over an unpleasant situation. **Rather than cry, find out what God's Word says concerning the situation and speak to it.** If God's Word gives you assurance concerning your situation, respond to it by speaking a related Word.

For he hath said, I will never leave thee, nor forsake thee.

Fourth Secret

So that we may boldly say, The Lord is my helper, and I will not fear what man shall do unto me.

Hebrews 13:5-6

In the above passage, God said that He will never leave us nor forsake us, so that we can boldly say that the Lord is our helper. Though God has said He will never leave us nor forsake, we still need to boldly say that He is our helper. When God's Word speaks to you, you have to boldly speak the promise into your life.

If you want your prayers to be effective, always speak to your situation. If you desire to be married, search the scripture and find out what the Bible says concerning your situation and start confessing it until you get married. For instance, you can take hold of the scripture that says, "none shall lack her mate" (Isaiah 34:16) and start speaking it into your life until you are married. If you have experienced disappointment in any area of life, you can take hold of the scripture that says "affliction can never arise a second time" (Nahum 1:9) and start speaking it. If you need healing, you can start confessing the scripture that says you are healed by the stripes of Jesus (1 Peter 2:24).

No matter what you desire, just find out what the Bible says concerning the situation and start confessing it. That way, you will definitely have whatever you desire. I make good use of this secret. I won't forget how I used this secret to salvage a situation we had at one of our seminars. The story will motivate you.

My Story

I was revealing deep mysteries of God at a seminar we held at the Exousia Dunamis, Lagos Nigeria on November 18, 2006 when something strange happened. The Word was with so much power at the seminar. And in the midst of the teaching, a lady sitting at the back of the hall suddenly stood up and charged with lightning speed towards the pulpit. As she charged towards the pulpit, she was making a lion-like noise. Her speed was so quick that the ushers couldn't stop her from getting to the pulpit.

I didn't see her until she was very close to me: few centimeters away. I suddenly noticed her running towards me with her two hands raised as if ready to strangle me. The speed was so quick that there was no way I could have avoided her from colliding with me. At that instant, a Word in Psalm 105:15 dropped in my heart and I spoke it with authority "touch not my anointed and do my prophet no harm". She immediately fell under the anointing as if there were no bones in her. I continued the teaching and ministered to her afterwards.

I didn't quite understand what she wanted to do to me, but it was very clear that her ultimate aim was to disrupt the powerful teaching. But because I spoke God's Word, she failed in disrupting the teaching. Speaking the Word is a powerful secret of prayer that helps us to change our unwanted situations.

Steps to Make your Spoken Word Effective

Although this secret of prayer is powerful, every spoken Word does not produce results. There are two steps that can make your spoken Word effective and powerful.

First Step

The first step of speaking an effective and powerful Word is to have a revelational knowledge of the Word. When you Speak a

Fourth Secret

revealed Word, it functions like the sword of the Spirit (Ephesians 6:17). The word becomes very powerful. To understand and have a revelational knowledge of the Word, you need to study the Bible verse by verse. You don't have to study 20 chapters of the Bible everyday unless you are writing an examination on Bible Knowledge. But if you are not writing any Bible Knowledge examination, I advise that you take your time and study the scripture. The Bible is not a novel that you read hurriedly. Study one verse everyday. If you don't understand a particular verse, it's important that you revisit it the next day and continue studying it until you understand it. Any verse you find difficult to understand may be the very verse that will help you to excel in life. **The more you study the Bible, the more you understand it. And the more you understand the Bible, the more powerful your spoken Word**.

Second Step

The second step is to believe the Word you speak. If one doesn't believe his spoken Word, it cannot produce results. Belief makes a spoken Word powerful. **When you believe your spoken Word, it automatically becomes a supernatural statement.** And because it has become supernatural, it must produce results. But when one confesses without believing his spoken Word, he is just making an empty noise. Belief precedes confession. You can only confess a particular scripture because you have already believed it. This explains why the Bible says that we first believed before speaking (2 Corinthians 4:13). So long as you believe the Word you speak, you will definitely achieve your desired goal. What then will make you believe your spoken Word?

Fourth Secret

The level of your belief determines whether you will believe your spoken Word or not. **When your belief is strengthened, you will easily believe your spoken Word. On the other hand, when your belief is weakened, you will not believe your spoken Word.** To strengthen your belief, put to use the four factors I explained in the third chapter. First, abstain from sin. Second, do not ask God for something evil. Third, do not pray with wrong motives. Finally, believe that God answers all your prayers.

No matter how bad your situation is, find out what God's Word says concerning the situation. When you discover it, understand and believe it, start confessing it, and your situation will surely change. It's a deep secret. Apart from the fact it's scriptural, it has been tested and proven. It works!

CHAPTER 6

FIFTH SECRET

Using the name of Jesus is another powerful secret that makes prayer successful. This secret of prayer produces amazing results, but it does not work for everyone. It only works for persons who are eligible to make use of His name. As long as you are eligible to make use of Jesus' name, every prayer you say in His name must produce results.

Unfortunately, majority of the persons who pray in the name of Jesus are ineligible to make use of His name. This explains why many persons pray in the name of Jesus and still don't have their hearts' desires. For any prayer you say in the name of Jesus to produce results, you have to be eligible to make use of His name.

Becoming Eligible to make use of Jesus' Name

Everyone does not have the right to make use of the name of Jesus. For you to be eligible to make use of His name, there are five steps you must take.

First step

The first step of becoming eligible to make use of Jesus' name is to know who He is. If Jesus is a stranger to you, then you are not qualified to pray in His name. You need to know Him before you can pray in His name. Who then is Jesus Christ?

Jesus Christ is God's Word that became flesh and dwelt on earth (John 1:14). His birth was a miracle, His life on earth was a miracle, His death was a miracle, and His resurrection was equally a miracle. He was conceived by the power of the Holy Ghost (Luke 1:35) and was born of a virgin: a young woman who had never had sex in her life.

While on earth, His life was a miracle. He raised the dead, opened blind eyes, healed the sick, made the lame walk, walked on water, fed 5,000 persons with five loaves of bread and two fish, and performed many other amazing miracles.

His death was also a miracle. On the day of His death, darkness fell upon the earth from 12 noon until 3 p.m. when the curtain of the temple that separated the holy of holies from the holy place was torn in half, from the top to the bottom. And He commended His spirit into the hands of the Father and died (Luke

Fifth Secret

23:44-46). This is amazing! Even as He was dying, He directed His spirit where to go.

His resurrection was equally a miracle. Before Jesus' death, He had said He would be raised from the dead after three days. So, after His death and burial, the chief priests and Pharisees demanded that Pilate should give instructions for Jesus' tomb to be sealed and guarded by soldiers to make sure Jesus' disciples wouldn't steal His body and claim He had risen. Pilate granted their request and the tomb was sealed with a great stone and guarded by heavily armed soldiers (Matthew 27:62-66). On the resurrection day, there was a great earthquake and the angel of the Lord came from heaven and rolled away the stone. When the guards saw the angel of the Lord whose countenance was like lightning, and whose raiment was as white as snow, they trembled and fainted (Matthew 28:1-4). Jesus resurrected in spite of the sealing of the tomb and the heavily armed soldiers. It's amazing!

After His resurrection, Jesus was given all authority in heaven and on earth (Matthew 28:18). He became the head of the church (Colossians 1:18) and also the head of all principalities and powers (Colossians 2:10). God equally exalted Jesus and gave Him a name above all names as such that by the mention of His name every knee should bow in heaven, on earth and beneath the earth, and every tongue should confess that He is Lord (Philippians 2:9-11). In heaven, Jesus is the master. On earth, He is the master, and beneath the earth, He is also the master. He is the master of the universe. Knowing Him is the first step of becoming eligible to make use of His name.

Second Step

The second step of becoming eligible to make use of Jesus' name is to have a cordial relationship with Him by becoming His disciple. You can't make use of His name without having a cordial relationship with Him. He did not permit everyone in the world to make use of His name. He only permitted His disciples. So, for you to be eligible to make use of His name, you must become His disciple. How do you become a disciple of Christ?

First, by receiving Christ: confessing that Jesus is Lord and believing that God raised Him from the dead (Romans 10:9). Second, by abstaining from sin. Receiving Christ is not enough to be His disciple. You have to continue obeying the Word before you can be His disciple (John 8:31). Those who commit sin are not His disciples. Such persons are of the devil (1 John 3:8).

Third Step

The third step of becoming eligible to make use of Jesus' name is to understand why we pray in His name. When one doesn't know the reason we pray in His name, he cannot be eligible to make use of the name. Why do we pray in the name of Jesus?

We pray in Jesus' name because He gave us the power of attorney to ask whatever we want in His name (John 14:13-14). In other words, He gave us the right to pray on His behalf. Anytime you pray in the name of Jesus, you are simply praying on behalf of Jesus. The prayer automatically becomes Jesus' prayer.

So, it's improper for you to be bothered anytime you pray in the name of Jesus. Though you will benefit from the prayer, it's Jesus' prayer because you said it in His name. And if it's truly Jesus' prayer, then nothing should worry you because He is the master of the universe. The prayer will surely produce results.

Fourth Step

The fourth step of becoming eligible to pray in Jesus' name is to have the revelational knowledge of the efficacy of His name. Apart from knowing why we pray in Jesus' name, you also need to understand and believe that the name of Jesus is the ultimate name that guarantees answers to prayers. When one lacks the knowledge of the efficacy of Jesus' name, he becomes ineligible to pray in His name. In God's Kingdom, anyone who lacks knowledge suffers (Hosea 4:6). So, when one lacks the knowledge of the efficacy of Jesus' name, his prayers may not produce results, even though he prays in the name of Jesus.

When Jesus gave us the power of attorney to make use of His name, He clearly stated that He would personally grant any request we would make in His name. In fact He said, "whatsoever you shall ask in my name, that I will do" (John 14:13). The word "whatsoever" means anything. There is absolutely no limit to what you can achieve when you pray in the name of Jesus, so long as you are eligible to make use of His name.

Fifth Step

The fifth step of becoming eligible to make use of Jesus' name is to be constantly conscious of the efficacy of the name of Jesus. Some persons are aware of the efficacy of the name of Jesus but are not always conscious of it. **Praying in the name of Jesus without being conscious of the efficacy of His name is the same thing as praying without knowing the efficacy of His name.** When one prays in the name of Jesus without being conscious of the efficacy of His name, his prayer may not produce results. To be eligible to make use of Jesus' name, you must be constantly conscious of the efficacy of His name.

If you follow the five steps above, you will become eligible to pray in Jesus' name. And no matter how far-fetched your desire seems to be, you will surely have it.

How Peter and John made use of Jesus' Name

The apostles of Christ were constantly conscious of the efficacy of the name of Jesus and they really made use of the name. One such instance was when Peter and John made use of the name to heal a man who was lame from his mother's womb (Acts 3: 1-8). Peter said to the man, "In the name of Jesus Christ of Nazareth rise up and walk", and the man became healed.

Peter didn't struggle in the prayer because he was conscious of the fact that Jesus gave us a power of attorney. He was not just conscious of it but very sure of it. And for that reason, he didn't waste time in his prayer: it was just a one-sentence prayer. Though it was a one-sentence prayer, it was very powerful because it was said in the name of Jesus.

I always teach about the efficacy of the name of Jesus at our seminars and the attendees of our seminars pray in the name of Jesus and record amazing testimonies. Leslie, an attendee of our seminar in England, made use of the name of Jesus to get a good job.

How Leslie made use of Jesus' Name

Leslie was between jobs when she attended a 2-Day seminar we held at the Excel Centre London England on Saturday July 23 and Sunday July 24, 2011. At the seminar, I talked

Fifth Secret

about the efficacy of the name of Jesus. She understood the teaching and prayed for a job in the name of Jesus. At the end of the seminar, she received a call from an organization offering her a job. Before she got home that same day, she got another job offer from another organization. It was really amazing.

She got two job offers on a Saturday. Organizations don't usually work on weekends how much more offering jobs on weekends. But because she used the name of Jesus to pray, she got two job offers that Saturday. That was really amazing! The organizations had to work on a Saturday evening because of her.

She understood that praying in the name of Jesus could help one achieve his goals. She made use of it, and it worked for her. If you make use of the name of Jesus, it will work for you as well. Ben made use of it at our Kumasi seminar and had an unbelievable financial testimony.

How Ben made use of Jesus' Name

Ben, who was the CEO of a company that was indebted to the tune of $250,000, attended our seminar at the 60,000-seater Baba Yara Stadium Kumasi Ghana on November 19 and 21, 2010. At the seminar, I taught about the efficacy of the name of Jesus. Ben prayed accordingly and had an unbelievable testimony.

Ben prayed for a solution to the company's debt. And few hours after, he received a phone call from an associate who promised to pay off the entire debt of $250,000. That was undoubtedly a huge miracle considering the amount of money. Such miracle took place because Ben prayed in the name of Jesus. Start making use of the name of Jesus and your prayers will produce amazing results.

Fifth Secret

Start Making Use of Jesus' Name

If you are truly a disciple of Christ, become constantly conscious of the power of attorney Jesus gave us. And no power can stop you from having whatever you desire, if you pray in His name. If you are not yet a disciple of Christ, become one by receiving Christ: confessing that Jesus is Lord and believing that God raised Him from the dead. And after receiving Christ, you are also required to abstain from sin.

I urge you to start making use of the name of Jesus from now onwards, and it will work for you. If it worked for Peter and John, then it will work for you because God is no respecter of persons (Acts 10:34). If it worked for Leslie and Ben, it will also work for you. Pray in the name of Jesus, the master of the universe, and you will surely have whatever your desire. It's a secret: a powerful secret of prayer.

CHAPTER 7

SIXTH SECRET

The sixth secret of prayer is forgiveness. This secret is a very delicate one mainly for two reasons. First, some people are not aware that unforgiveness stops prayers from producing results. Second, many unforgiving persons are not aware that they are unforgiving.

Unforgiveness hinders Prayers from Producing Results

God doesn't answer an unforgiving person's prayer. When one bears a grudge, his prayers will not produce results. The truth is that an unforgiving person is not even qualified to pray. For your prayers to produce results, you must first forgive those who sin against you.

> Therefore I say unto you, What things soever ye desire, when ye pray, believe that ye receive them, and ye shall have them.
>
> And when ye stand praying, forgive, if ye have ought against any: that your Father also which is in heaven may forgive you your trespasses.
>
> Mark 11:24-25

In verse 24 above, Jesus revealed a condition of successful prayer. He said that we will have whatever we desire, provided that we pray believing. Then verse 25 starts with the conjunction "and", which means that verse 25 is a continuation of the condition of successful prayer that Jesus revealed in verse 24. And in the verse 25, Jesus said that before we pray, we should forgive those who offend us so that Our Father will forgive us our sins. The first lesson to learn from verse 25 is that God will forgive us our sins only if we forgive those who offend us. The second lesson to learn from the verse is that Jesus wants all our sins to be forgiven before we can be eligible to make any prayer request. **Yes, the forgiveness of one's sins is a criterion for the success of the person's prayer.**

When one receives Christ as his Lord and savior, He receives the gift of righteousness (Romans 5:17), and all his sins are forgiven. The person will then be required to abstain from sin and forgive those who offend him. If he doesn't forgive anyone who offends him, God will cancel the forgiveness of his sins

Sixth Secret

and recall the sins (Matthew 18:21-35). When the person's sins are recalled, he ceases to be righteous and his prayers can no longer be effective. For your prayers to produce results, you must be righteous. It's only the righteous person's prayer that produces results (James 5:16).

You must learn to forgive everyone who offends you. **You are not doing a person a favor by forgiving him. Rather, it's a medium for God to forgive your own sins.** And when your sins are forgiven, God sees you as a righteous person and your prayers will then produce results. So, forgiving others is for your own good. No matter what a person does to you, forgive the person from your heart and your prayers will produce results.

Understanding why Unforgiveness hinders Prayers

In Christianity, we are under a commandment to forgive everyone. **It's not compulsory to be a Christian but if you choose to become one, you must forgive everyone who offends you.** Before the coming of Jesus Christ, revenge was permitted and forgiveness wasn't compulsory. But when Jesus came, He changed it and forgiveness became compulsory.

> Ye have heard that it hath been said, An eye for an eye, and a tooth for a tooth:
>
> But I say unto you, That ye resist not evil: but whosoever shall smite thee on thy right cheek, turn to him the other also.
> Matthew 5:38-39

Before the coming of Jesus, the Law of Moses permitted revenge but Jesus changed it in the passage above. Rather than an eye for an eye, Jesus said we should not "resist evil". In other words, rather than revenge, Jesus said we should forgive. Because of the change, anyone who doesn't forgive from his heart has no relationship with God. Jesus actually said that God would deal with such person (Matthew 18:35). For that reason, the person's prayer cannot produce results. It's only the prayer of the righteous person that produces results (James 5:16). And an unforgiving person is not righteous because the forgiveness of his sin has been cancelled and his sins recalled (Matthew 18:21-35).

Prayer Against an Enemy connotes Unforgiveness

Any person who prays against someone is an

unforgiving person, and should not expect his prayers to produce results. In fact, Jesus said that such person is not a child of God.

Ye have heard that it hath been said, Thou shalt love thy neighbour, and hate thine enemy.

But I say unto you, Love your enemies, bless them that curse you, do good to them that hate you, and pray for them which despitefully use you, and persecute you;

That ye may be the children of your Father which is in heaven: for he maketh his sun to rise on the evil and on the good, and sendeth rain on the just and on the unjust.

> Matthew 5:43-45

Sixth Secret

Before the coming of Jesus, it was proper to hate enemies and this explains why King David wrote so many prayers against his enemies in the Book of Psalms. Even in the Book of Exodus, the Bible says we should not suffer a witch to live (Exodus 22:18). Then, it was very proper to hate enemies. But in the passage above, Jesus changed it and said we should start loving our enemies.

Jesus also said in the scripture that we should bless those who curse us, be nice to those who hate us, and pray for those who persecute us so that we will be the children of our heavenly Father. In other words, you are a child of our heavenly Father when you love your enemies, bless those who curse you, be nice to those who hate you, and pray for those who persecute you. **It also means that anyone who prays against his enemies is not a child of God.**

Cursing People hinders Prayers

Christianity is not a joke! If you want to be a Christian, you must love everyone. You must not curse or pray against anyone. **The mouth of a Christian should only be used for blessings: to bless God and human beings.** When a Christian curses or prays against someone, the Christian's mouth is automatically defiled, and his prayers can no longer produce results. Apostle James explained it well.

> But the tongue can no man tame; it is an unruly evil, full of deadly poison.

> Therewith bless we God, even the Father; and therewith curse we men, which are made after the similitude of God.

Sixth Secret

Out of the same mouth proceedeth blessing and cursing. My brethren, these things ought not so to be.

Doth a fountain send forth at the same place sweet water and bitter?

Can the fig tree, my brethren, bear olive berries? either a vine, figs? so can no fountain both yield salt water and fresh.
James 3:8-12

A mouth can either be used to bless or to curse. Just like no fountain has the ability to produce both salt and fresh water, no mouth can be used for both blessings and curses. **If you want your prayers to produce results, bless all and curse none.** When you curse, you automatically lose the ability to bless. If you are a pastor, and you want your prayers to produce results when you pray for people, bless everyone and curse no one.

Vengeance is the Exclusive Responsibility of God

It's necessary I let you know that no evil can befall you when you pray for your enemy. Don't feel that your enemy will kill you if you pray for him. On the contrary, when you are nice to your enemy and pray for him, God will take over your battle and fight on your behalf (Romans 12:19). Vengeance actually belongs to God. But for Him to avenge on your behalf, you must not avenge yourself. **When you take revenge against your enemy, God leaves room for you to fight the battle yourself, but when you are nice to your enemy, you leave room for God's wrath to fight on your behalf** (Romans 12:19 NIV). And because no one can fight against

God, the Bible likens it to heaping coals of fire on your enemy's head (Romans 12:20). **The Bible does not say there is no vengeance. Rather, the Bible wants you to know that vengeance is God's sole prerogative.**

So many persons struggle and suffer in life today because they avenge themselves. If you want to excel in life, forgive everyone and pray against no one, and your prayers will surely produce results. Ifeyinwa's testimony will shock you.

Ifeyinwa's Testimony

Ifeyinwa left secondary school in 1994 and graduated from the university in the year 2000. After her university education, she desired two things: to get a good job, and to get married. But the two things eluded her. No one was really interested in marrying her. She experienced delayed marriage. She was not able to get a job as well. She didn't have money to take care of her basic needs as a woman. She really struggled in life. She continued struggling until February 15, 2014 when she attended our seminar at Sharon Hall Onitsha Nigeria.

At the seminar, I taught extensively about forgiveness, and Ifeyinwa understood the teaching. She then forgave everyone who offended her. Instead of praying against her enemies, she decided to pray for them. And she had a shocking testimony.

When Ifeyinwa got home that night, she was tired and went to sleep almost immediately. At 3 a.m., a phone call woke her up. When she picked the call, she demanded to know who the caller was as the caller's number wasn't saved on her phone. The caller identified herself as her secondary school mate whom she hadn't seen for over 19 years. "How did you get my number", Ifeyinwa asked. "I got it

Sixth Secret

from your brother. I just phoned him before calling you. Ifeyinwa, I have a confession to make", she said.

To Ifeyinwa's shock, she confessed that she placed a curse on her when they were in secondary school because Ifeyinwa bullied her on one occasion. She explained to Ifeyinwa that she had been troubled for the past nine hours. She said that the only way she could be herself was to confess to Ifeyinwa. And that was why she couldn't wait for daybreak before calling. She told Ifeyinwa she had cancelled the curse. She apologized and pleaded for her forgiveness.

Ifeyinwa had such a shocking testimony because she forgave all her enemies and prayed for them. As long as she prayed against her enemies, she wasn't a child of God (Matthew 5:43-45). But when she attended our seminar, she forgave her enemies and prayed for them. And God took over her battle. This explains why her secondary school mate, who placed a curse on her over 19 years ago, became troubled at the same time she prayed for her enemies. If you forgive those who offend you and pray for your enemies, God will take over your battle, and your enemies will be in trouble. Your prayers will also produce results. Seyi's amazing testimony will equally shock you.

Seyi's Testimony

Seyi had never had any marriage proposal before attending our seminar at the Eko Hotel and Suites Lagos Nigeria in August 2011. The seminar was a 2-Day seminar: on Saturday August 13, 2011 and Sunday August 14, 2011. On the first day of the seminar, she learnt about forgiveness and forgave everyone who offended her. She also prayed for her enemies, and she had many astonishing marriage proposals.

Sixth Secret

When Seyi got home on that fateful day, one of her old friends called her on phone and proposed marriage to her. As she finished talking with him, another friend of hers called and proposed as well. After speaking with the second suitor, she received yet another marriage proposal from another caller. She continued receiving different marriage proposals on phone. And by 12 noon the next day, she had had seven marriage proposals from seven different men.

The next day, which was the last day of the seminar, I made alter call for testimonies, and Seyi came out. While she was still standing in front of the podium, she received the eighth marriage proposal via text message. And she became scared. Eight marriage proposals within 24 hours! It was really astonishing!

Seyi had such astonishing testimony because she forgave those who offended her and prayed for them. As long as she prayed against her enemies, her prayers couldn't produce results. But the moment she forgave and stopped praying against her enemies, she had astonishing marriage proposals.

I enjoin you to stop praying against people. Don't curse anyone. Forgive everyone who offends you and your prayers will produce wonderful results. It's a secret that has been tested and proven. It works!

CHAPTER 8

SEVENTH SECRET

The seventh secret that makes prayer successful is thanksgiving. This secret opens the Father's heart to grant seemingly impossible prayer requests. Thanksgiving is very important but is not well valued in this dispensation. Presently, we have a category of persons who feel that they don't have any reason to be grateful to the Father. In fact, some persons in this category are even angry that the Father has not met some of their needs. We also have another category of persons who realize that there is a need to thank the Father, but the Father doesn't accept some of their thanksgiving because they don't go about it the right way.

The Father does not accept all thanksgiving. There are some conditions of successful thanksgiving. But before revealing the conditions, it's important that you first understand some basic principles of thanksgiving.

What is Thanksgiving?

Thanksgiving can be defined as an expression of gratitude. When you are grateful to God for what He has done for you, then He does more. I know that you may have some unmet needs but the truth is that there are some of your needs that are already met. If you are grateful to God for meeting those needs, then He will meet your other needs.

Thanksgiving opens God's heart in a very easy and shocking manner. If you have been asking the Father for a particular thing for a long time and you haven't seen the result, stop asking and start thanking Him. If God accepts your thanksgiving, you will have your heart's desire easily. **Thanksgiving is a very powerful secret that will help you achieve your goals.** It will even help you achieve seemingly impossible goals. Jesus Christ used it to perform seemingly impossible miracles.

Jesus used Thanksgiving to perform Seemingly Impossible Miracles

Thanksgiving opens God's heart to grant seemingly impossible prayer requests. It touches God's heart in an unbelievable manner. Jesus Christ made use of this powerful secret to perform seemingly impossible miracles. He used it to raise Lazarus from the dead four days after his death.

Then they took away the stone from the place where the dead was laid. And Jesus lifted up his eyes, and said, **Father, I thank thee that thou hast heard me.**

And I knew that thou hearest me always: but because of the people which stand by I said it, that they may believe that thou hast sent me.

And when he thus had spoken, he cried with a loud voice, Lazarus, come forth.

And he that was dead came forth, bound hand and foot with graveclothes: and his face was bound about with a napkin. Jesus saith unto them, Loose him, and let him go.

> John 11:41-44

Seventh Secret

Raising Lazarus from the dead wasn't an ordinary miracle because he was dead for four days, and his body was already rotten and stinking (John 11:39). Raising one from the dead one hour after his death is a big miracle, but raising Lazarus from the dead four days after his death was a much bigger miracle because his body was already rotten. It was indeed one of the greatest miracles Jesus performed. How did He perform this great miracle? He simply gave thanks to the Father and called Lazarus. Though the prayer sounded simple, it was a very powerful prayer. The thanksgiving opened God's heart, and the miracle that seemed impossible took place easily. Thanksgiving opens God's heart to grant seemingly impossible prayer requests. Jesus also used thanksgiving to perform another seemingly impossible miracle when He fed 5,000 persons with just five loaves of bread and two small fish.

There is a lad here, which hath five barley loaves, and two small fishes: but what are they among so many?

And Jesus said, Make the men sit down. Now there was much grass in the place. So the men sat down, in number about five thousand.

And Jesus took the loaves; and **when he had given thanks**, he distributed to the disciples, and the disciples to them that were set down; and likewise of the fishes as much as they would.

When they were filled, he said unto his disciples, Gather up the fragments that remain, that nothing be lost.

Therefore they gathered them together, and filled twelve baskets with the

Seventh Secret

fragments of the five barley loaves, which remained over and above unto them that had eaten.

John 6:9-13

In the above scripture, Jesus fed 5,000 persons with five loaves of bread and two small fish. And when they were filled, they had 12 baskets full of bread fragments remaining. Undoubtedly, it was a seemingly impossible miracle. To perform the miracle, all He did was to give thanks to the Father.

Giving thanks to the Father touches His heart to grant seemingly impossible prayer requests. Jesus never struggled when he was on earth. Anytime He encountered a seemingly impossible situation, He would simply give thanks to the Father and the miracle would manifest. If you want to achieve seemingly impossible goals, then always give thanks to the Father.

Use Thanksgiving to make Requests to the Father

I admonish you to start using thanksgiving to make requests to the Father. It will really help you receive answers to your prayers. Apostle Paul admonished the Philippians similarly.

> Be careful for nothing; but in every thing by prayer and supplication with thanksgiving let your requests be made known unto God.
>
> Philippians 4:6

In the above scripture, Apostle Paul advised the Philippians never to worry about anything. He said to them that instead of worrying, they should use thanksgiving to make request to God. Do not worry any longer. Instead of worrying, use thanksgiving to make request to the Father.

Have you realized that anytime you give someone a gift and he appreciates it so much, you always feel like giving him another gift? The same thing is applicable to God. **The more grateful you are to God, the more blessings He releases to you**. I once gave a gift of some of my used clothes to two brothers in Christ, and they were both grateful. But one of them was exceptionally grateful. He expressed his gratitude in a very remarkable way that made me happy and fulfilled. And that made me to give him more clothes, including new ones.

If we, the children of God, are happy when people are grateful to us, then our heavenly Father is indeed very happy when we are grateful to Him. Do you know that when your thanksgiving touches the Father's heart, He will ask you to request for anything you need?

King Solomon's Testimony

King Solomon offered 1,000 burnt offerings to thank God for making him a king and God demanded that he should ask for anything.

And the king went to Gibeon to sacrifice there; for that was the great high place: a thousand burnt offerings did Solomon offer upon that altar.

In Gibeon the LORD appeared to Solomon in a dream by night: **and God said, Ask what I shall give thee.**

1Kings 3:4-5

King Solomon was grateful to God for making him a king and God said to him "Ask what I shall give thee". God asked him to send his prayer requests. God hasn't changed, beloved. If your gratitude touches His heart,

"He will ask you to send your prayer requests". Martha's gratitude touched God's heart when she attended our seminar, and "God asked her to send her prayer requests".

Martha's Testimony

Martha is a Nigerian lady who desired to marry a white man. She attended our seminar at the Eko Hotel and Suites Lagos Nigeria on August 13 and 14, 2011. At the seminar, she gave a sacrificial offering that touched God's heart, and she had her desired testimony. Shortly after the seminar, she met a white English man she liked so much. Few months later, the man proposed, and they got married in 2012.

Martha was grateful to God for making it possible for her to marry the English man. And she decided to attend our seminar in December 2012 to thank God. The seminar took place at Haven Event Centre Lagos Nigeria on December 6, 2012. At the seminar, she gave a thanksgiving offering appreciating God for her wedding. Her thanksgiving went before God as a sweet smelling savor, and she asked God for a child. She became pregnant immediately after the seminar. And nine months later, she was delivered of twins: a boy and a girl.

Martha had such amazing testimony because she gave a thanksgiving offering to God for making it possible for her to marry the man of her dreams. You must develop a heart of gratitude. You must specially thank God anytime He does something for you. True thanksgiving opens the Father's heart to perform amazing miracles. But I must warn that every thanksgiving does not open the Father's heart. For your thanksgiving to be accepted, there are two conditions you must meet.

Conditions of Successful Thanksgiving

God does not accept every thanksgiving. For Him to accept your thanksgiving, there are two conditions you must meet.

First Condition

The very first condition is to abstain from sin. You must abstain from sin before your thanksgiving will be accepted. Everyone is not eligible to give thanksgiving to the Father. Only righteous persons are eligible to give thanksgiving to the Father. A sinner is not qualified to give thanksgiving to the Father. In fact, the Bible says that the sacrifice of a sinner is an abomination (Proverbs 15:8).

It's important you note that a sinner is a sinner, whether he goes to church or not. Though righteousness is a gift, no sinner can be righteous. If one receives Christ and still commits sin, then he is a sinner. This explains why the Bible says that he who does what is right is righteous and he who commits sin is of the devil (1 John 3:7-8). So, if you want your thanksgiving to be accepted, you must abstain from sin.

Second Condition

The second condition is to be grateful to God for the things He has done in your life. When one is not appreciative, God doesn't accept his thanksgiving. Thanksgiving means an expression of gratitude. So, when one thanks the Father without any gratitude, it's not regarded as thanksgiving. Thanksgiving must come from your heart. You must be genuinely grateful to the Father for the things He has done in your life. When you are genuinely grateful to the Father, He accepts your thanksgiving.

Seventh Secret

Many people are busy complaining and asking God for one thing or the other without thanking Him for their needs He has already met. Rather than complain about the things God hasn't done for you, be genuinely grateful to Him for the ones He has done and He will do the rest. Anytime you pray, first thank Him for the things He has done before asking for more. I advise you to sing praises to our heavenly Father from time to time, and thank Him for your needs He has met. You can even thank Him for your unmet needs.

If you abstain from sin and genuinely thank Him from your heart, your prayers will produce results. It's a very powerful secret!

CHAPTER 9

THE MOST POWERFUL PROTECTION PRAYER POINT

The seven secrets of prayer won't be complete without revealing the most important protection prayer point on earth. Below is the prayer point.

> Heavenly Father, please deliver me from evil in Jesus name.

The prayer point above looks simple but it's the most powerful protection prayer point that exists. How can asking God to deliver you from evil be the most powerful protection prayer point? The reason is simple. The devil and his agents don't have the power to attack a child of God, provided that the child of God abstains from sin (1 John 5:18). But when a child of God commits a sin that leads to death, the devil will then have power to attack the person. There are sins that lead to death and there are sins that do not lead to death.

> If you see any brother or sister commit a sin that does not lead to death, you should pray and God will give them life. I refer to those whose sin does not lead to death. There is a sin that leads to death. I am not saying that you should pray about that.
>
> All wrongdoing is sin, and there is sin that does not lead to death.
>
> 1 John 5:16-17(NIV)

The above scripture clarifies the fact that we have some sins that lead to death and some sins that don't lead to death. The death referred to in the passage is spiritual death and not physical death. Some of the sins that lead to death are sexual immorality, impurity, debauchery, idolatry, witchcraft, hatred, discord, jealousy, fits of rage, and selfish ambition (Galatians 5:19-21).

When one commits a sin that leads to death, he dies spiritually and the Holy Spirit departs from him. Whenever the Holy Spirit departs from a person, such person loses his relationship with the Father (Romans 8:9). And the devil or any of his agents can then attack him. What that means is that as long as you don't commit a sin that leads to death, the devil or his agents cannot attack you.

How then can you avoid committing a sin that leads to death? The only means you can avoid committing a sin that leads to death is by resisting the temptation of the devil. This therefore makes it extremely necessary for you to ask the Father to deliver you from evil. If He delivers you from evil temptations, then you cannot commit a sin that leads to death, and your relationship with Him will be intact. As a result of that, the devil and his agents cannot have power over you.

Though the devil does not have the right to attack a child of God, he has the right to tempt him. And he knows that when a child of God commits a sin that leads to death, he ceases to be a child of God. For that reason, the devil focuses on tempting children of God with sins that lead to death. If a child of God falls into the temptation and commits a sin that leads to death, he automatically ceases to be a child of God, and can then be attacked by the devil. **As long as you don't fall into any evil temptation, you won't commit a sin that leads to death, and the devil cannot attack you.**

And the best way to avoid falling into an evil temptation is to ask the Father to deliver you from evil. It's a powerful prayer point. Jesus also taught us a similar prayer point.

> And lead us not into temptation, but deliver us from evil.
>
> Matthew 6:13

In the above scripture, Jesus taught us to ask Our Father to deliver us from evil. If you go through the Lord's Prayer, you will realize that there is just one protection prayer point, which is, to ask our heavenly Father to deliver us from evil. **If asking Our Father to deliver us from evil is the only protection prayer point in the Lord's Prayer, it means that the prayer point is strong enough to protect us.** It means that it's a powerful prayer point. It also means that it's God's responsibility to deliver us from evil. **When the Father takes**

over the responsibility of delivering you from evil, you can never fall into any evil temptation. Even when you unknowingly want to commit a sin, God will show up and will somehow prevent you from committing the sin. Judas Iscariot betrayed Jesus because he fell into an evil temptation (John 13:2). The devil also planned to "sift Peter like a wheat" but Jesus prayed for him (Luke 22:31-32).

Always ask Our Father to deliver you from evil. For Jesus to teach us to ask Our Father to deliver us from evil simply means that Jesus really wants us to always say the prayer point. It's the most powerful protection prayer point on earth. **For the mere fact that this prayer point came from Jesus connotes that it must be good enough for Christians.** Jesus is Our Lord and knows what's best for us. He also prayed a similar prayer point for His disciples shortly before Judas betrayed him.

> I pray not that thou shouldest take them out of the world, but that thou shouldest keep them from the evil.
>
> John 17:15

In the above scripture, Jesus prayed that our heavenly Father shouldn't take His disciples out of the world but rather keep them from the evil one. If the Father keeps you from evil or from the evil one, then no evil can affect you.

Never you be scared of the devil. Just make sure you ask the Father to deliver you from evil and that's it. The prayer point protects you completely from the devil, demons, witches, the devil's agents, and from all kinds of evil.

I must warn that this prayer point will only work in your life if you have an intimate relationship with the Father. To have an intimate relationship with the Father, you must first receive Christ in your life, and abstain from sin. **When you indulge in sin, you become vulnerable to the devil's attack, whether you pray or not. On the other hand, when you abstain from sin and do good things, you cannot be harmed by anyone (1 Peter 3:13).**

Our Father is the most powerful being that exists. So, asking Him to protect you is undoubtedly the most powerful protection prayer point. When He protects you, you can be sure of real protection. If you ask him to deliver you from evil, He will certainly protect you from all forms of evil, provided that you abstain from sin.

CHAPTER 10

MY ADVICE

If you want your prayers to produce results, you must completely abstain from sin. **No one who prays commits sin, and no one who commits sin prays.** You cannot do the two at the same time. One of the greatest deceits of the devil is to make people believe that they can do the two at the same time. But how can it be possible? Just like you can't eat your cake and still have it, you can't indulge in sin and still receive answers to your prayers. **Anyone who commits sin is not eligible to pray (Proverbs 28:9).** This explains why all the seven secrets of prayer require one to abstain from sin before he can be eligible to use them. That's is just the simple truth. **A sinner is not permitted to make a prayer request. A sinner who attends church services is equally not eligible to pray.** A person who indulges in sin after receiving Christ is still not eligible to pray. That you have received Christ does not give you the liberty to commit sin. Even grace does not give you the liberty to commit sin (Romans 6:15-16). If you have truly received Christ, then you must do good things like Christ (1 John 3:7).

If you have genuinely received Christ, you will abstain from sin. It's not possible to have Christ and be sinning at the same time. Anyone who commits sin is of the devil (1 John 3:8), and such person is not eligible to pray. I advise you to completely abstain from sin. **Even if you don't want to abstain from sin for paradise's sake, you must abstain from**

sin for your prayers to produce results. It's only the prayer of the righteous that produces results (James 5:16). Prayer was created only for the righteous: those who have intimate relationship with the Father. And for you to have an intimate relationship with the Father, you must first receive Christ (John 1:12), and abstain from sin. So long as you have an intimate relationship with the Father, make use of the seven secrets and your prayers will surely produce results.

If you want to receive answers to your prayers, you must forgive everyone who offends you. You can't have an intimate relationship with the Father without forgiving those who offend you. If you don't forgive others, the Father won't forgive your sins (Matthew 6:14-15). And if your sins are not forgiven, then you don't have an intimate relationship with Him. In fact the Bible says that if a person refuses to forgive his brother,

My Advice

the Father will cancel the forgiveness of his sins, recall his sins, and punish him (Matthew 18:21-35). So, you must forgive everyone who offends you before you can have an intimate relationship with the Father. You must forgive everyone, including your enemies. You must not pray against your enemies. Rather, pray for them. It will surely help you to have an intimate relationship with the Father, and your prayers will produce amazing results.

If you are truly a child of God, then address Him as Father when you pray. By addressing Him as Father, you remind Him of His intimate father-child relationship with you, which will in turn propel Him to answer your prayers.

If you really want your prayers to produce results, you must be constantly conscious of the fact that the Father answers all your prayers, as long as you pray believing (Mark 11:24). The consciousness will help strengthen your belief, which will in turn empower your prayers to produce results.

Finally, if you have understood the seven secrets, then you have to start making use of them now. The seven secrets are very powerful! Apart from the fact that the secrets are scriptural, they have all been tested and proven. They are very effective! However, I advise that you study this book every now and then. The more you study the book, the more you understand the secrets. And the more you understand the secrets, the more amazing results your prayers will produce. No matter what you desire, make use of the secrets and you will surely have your heart's desires in the mighty name of Jesus Christ.

Shalom and God's blessings to you!

SHARE YOUR TESTIMONY

If you have fully understood the seven secrets of prayer, I have no doubt that your prayers will produce wonderful results. I will like to rejoice with you and give thanks to Our Father for the impact the book has made in your life. Kindly email me your testimonies and praise reports at info@singlesandmarried.org

OTHER BOOKS BY CHRIS OJIGBANI

Relationship Secrets 101
Relationship Secrets 201
Relationship Secrets 322
Spiritual Warfare
I Want To Marry You
Back To Sender: Is It The Will Of God?
(Second Edition)
Resetting The Time Of Your Miracle
Activating The Grace Of Marriage

To order any of Chris Ojigbani's books, visit amazon.com, amazon.co.uk or call any of the numbers below:
Europe +44 757 655 4405,
Ghana +233 241 026 890,
Nigeria +234 806 285 9890
You can also send an email to info@singlesandmarried.org